SHAKES, QUAKES, AND SHIFTS

SHAKES, QUAKES, AND SHIFTS

EARTH TECTONICS

FRANKLYN M. BRANLEY   Illustrated by Daniel Maffia

Thomas Y. Crowell Company   New York

Manufactured in the United States of America

Library of Congress Cataloging in Publication Data

Branley, Franklyn Mansfield, 1915–
  Shakes, quakes, and shifts.

  SUMMARY: Briefly describes the continual changes that take
place within the earth and on its surface.
  Bibliography: p.
  1. Earth—Juv. lit. [1. Earth] I. Maffia, Daniel, illus. II. Title.
QB631.B697 1974 551 73-18059
ISBN 0-690-00422-2 ISBN 0-690-00423-0 (lib. bdg.)

2   3   4   5   6   7   8   9   10

Earth is restless.

Our planet is always moving, and always changing in many different ways. It rotates on its axis, revolves around the sun, and travels among the stars with the sun and other planets of our solar system. Tidal forces pull upon both land and sea. It is buffeted by the solar wind. Pictures of the earth taken by astronauts reveal that shifting patterns of clouds cover a large part of its seas and continents. Clouds are evidence of changing weather—storm systems that generally move along regular paths bringing rain, snow, sleet, and hail to the regions below.

MARS

MERCURY

VENUS

EARTH

No matter where you live you are aware of day-to-day weather changes. But there are also long-term weather changes that we cannot experience; they take too long to occur. The primary cause of weather is uneven heating of the earth. Since most of our heat comes from the sun, that star is the main cause of weather. During the millions of years that the sun has been shining there have been changes in the amount of energy it has produced—sudden increases as well as decreases. Therefore, at times during the history of our planet there have been major changes in earth's weather patterns. Tropical plants once grew in regions now covered with ice and snow; blankets of ice and snow a hundred feet thick and more once covered the farmlands of North America, Europe, and Asia.

The air has changed, too. It has evolved through millions of years to its present composition, mainly nitrogen and oxygen. Varying amounts of water vapor, dust, and pollen grains are added to it in different parts of the earth. All of these are important factors in the process of cloud formation and rainmaking. In addition, waste products from furnaces and factories and from oil and gasoline engines are spewed into the air. Many of these materials drop out of the air eventually. As the atmosphere blows and churns about, waste products are spread thinly through it; they are diluted. There are some five quadrillion (5,000,000,000,000,000) tons of air surrounding the earth. It can, and does, absorb tremendous amounts of waste gases.

When fuel is burned, carbon dioxide is released along with other waste gases. Some scientists believe that man-made carbon dioxide in the atmosphere may eventually become dense enough to make a sort of mirror that will reflect solar radiation, preventing it from reaching the surface. If this should happen, the temperature of the earth would drop. Only a slight decrease would be sufficient to bring about another ice age. Perhaps the early ice ages resulted from this same cause, as some people believe, except that in those days the carbon dioxide came

3

from volcanoes rather than from engines and furnaces. Others contend that if a carbon dioxide layer formed and persisted long enough, it would cause our planet to heat up rather than cool down. They agree that less solar radiation would reach earth. But whatever radiation did penetrate the carbon dioxide layer would be trapped; it could not escape into space. According to this theory, the heat would build up over the centuries, raising the temperature a hundred degrees or more over present levels. The high temperature of the surface of Venus (some 800°F.), the scientists point out, is probably due to the entrapping of heat by that planet's atmospheric blanket.

The air ocean around us and above us is always changing; from day to day, from century to century and through the thousands and millions of years our planet has existed. So also is the land we live on. You can see changes all around you. A swamp you know may once have been a pond. A small brook may have become a large stream, or it may no longer exist. Hay fields may now be overgrown with brush and small trees. A swamp may now be a shopping center, and a hillside once wooded may have become a housing development. There may be a flat beach where sand dunes stood as sentinels against the sea.

Man changes the surface of the land. But it is changed naturally too. Rain wears down jagged cliffs. Streams cut through solid rock; waves pounding the shores cut out new beaches; ocean currents shift millions of tons of sand from one location to another. Volcanoes build the earth's surface upward as the hot lava and cinders brought from the interior of the earth spread over the land, changing it

4

drastically. Entire new islands may be created when a volcano erupts under the sea.

Of all the natural causes of change in the surface of the earth, the most widespread and continuous is the action of water; the pounding of seas, the flowing of streams, and the falling of rain. And water itself is always changing. The atmosphere contains large amounts of water. Often you cannot see it because it is water vapor—an invisible gas. The water becomes visible and active in wearing down the land when it changes to rain, snow, hail, dew, or frost; it may be fresh water or salt, pure or polluted, liquid or solid.

Water dissolves minerals in rocks and soil. Given enough time, water will dissolve just about everything. Because it dissolves so many different substances, water is often called the universal solvent. That's one way that water wears away earth's surface. Also, water flows. Provided there is even the slightest difference in elevation, water will flow from one place to another. As it flows, water carries along everything that is in the water, or on top of it. Fast-moving water picks up mud and silt, sand, pebbles, and even rocks. When water slows down, it cannot carry as much material. The soil, sand, and rocks drop to the bottom. Century after century a mud plain builds up. Eventually new land is formed—rivers take land from one place and deposit it at another location. Deltas, new land masses, are built where rivers flow into the sea; the Nile delta in the Mediterranean Sea, the Mississippi delta in the Gulf of Mexico, and the Amazon delta in the Atlantic Ocean. Rivers are land movers.

Earth is a moving, restless, ever-changing planet. Many of the changes are made by man. Some of these changes are good: levees to keep rivers from flooding, lakes to store water, barriers to slow erosion by the sea. Many changes are harmful: the stripping of earth's surface to mine coal, copper, and other minerals; the filling of salt marshes to make new land for homes at the seashore; the leveling of fields and forests to make roads, freeways, and shopping centers. The most extensive changes in earth occur naturally. They are gigantic and cannot be controlled. Let's explore this planet of ours to get a look at some of them.

Only a few hundred years ago most people believed that the earth was flat. Ships did not venture far out to sea. Mariners feared that if they did, their ship might fall off the edge of the earth and disappear forever.

Today we are certain that earth is round. Men have seen the whole earth from outer space. Astronauts have taken pictures of earth from spaceships and from the moon. It is a ball covered by clouds. Occasionally the clouds are broken. Then one can see through them to the blue waters that make the Atlantic and Pacific and the other oceans that cover three-fourths of the earth and altogether make "the world ocean." We can see the continents that are in this ocean.

Of all the planets in our solar system, we've seen the surface of only two—our own earth and the planet Mars. There are no oceans on Mars, no clouds in its atmosphere. Mars appears to be a barren, desolate world. The other planets may be also. We've never seen the surface of Venus for it is covered by dense clouds which no camera can penetrate. Its surface remains a mystery. The surfaces of Jupiter, Saturn, Uranus, and Neptune also elude our exploration because of dense atmospheres. Pluto has no atmosphere that blocks our view, yet we cannot see details on the planet; it is too far away. As revealed by Mariner, Mercury is covered with craters, like those on the moon.

Earth appears to be the only planet that has continents in an all-surrounding sea. It is unique in the solar system.

No matter where you are on earth you can see very little of it. Your view covers only a few miles, and thus to earth dwellers today, as to the people of hundreds of years ago, our planet still seems to be flat. You can't see its roundness. Also, you can have no clue to what it's like underneath the surface.

Suppose we could slice right through the earth-ball, cut it in half as we might cut an orange. We would see that the planet is made up of layers.

The whole earth is about 7,900 miles in diameter. At the

CRUST

MANTLE

OUTER CORE

INNER CORE

very center of the earth there is a core of metal, mostly iron and nickel, we think. This core is probably 4,200 miles across. The inside of the core, about 1,600 miles across, is solid because of the great mass that pushes upon it. This pressure also makes the metal hot, but not hot enough to melt. Because it is pushed together so tightly, its melting temperature is very high.

The outer part of the core is liquid metal. Pressure is less here, so the metal isn't pushed together so tightly and it gets hot enough to melt. The layer isn't liquid like water; but the metal isn't solid either. It probably slips a bit, rubbing against the solid, rotating earth. Above the core is a layer called the mantle of the earth. At the bottom of this layer, metal and rock are melted together, forming the magma. The mixture changes to solid rock as the distance from the center of the earth increases. Above it lie the continents with their plains and high mountains, the islands, and the bottom of the sea. These make up the crust of the earth. It is a layer only 10 to 20 miles thick in most places. Parts of it may go down 25 to 30 miles but not much more. Deeper down, at 40 to 60 miles, the rocks merge into the magma. This is the surface on which the crust floats.

The mantle is not one unbroken layer that goes all around the earth. Huge pieces larger than whole continents move on top of the almost liquid rock. They don't move much, only about an inch a year. But in a million years that adds up to a million inches, and a million inches is almost 20 miles. Geologists believe that these masses have been moving 150 million years, or more. That means some continents have moved 3,000 miles.

Long ago, perhaps 200 million years ago— Before we go any further, let's think about time for a moment, and about generations of people. A generation covers about 25 years. By the time you're 25 years old, you'll probably have children. When they're 25, they will have children, and so on. In a hundred years there will be four generations. (Often people marry when they are very young, so there might be four or even five generations in less than 100 years.) In a thousand years that would mean 40 generations, and lots of great, great, great (and so on) grandparents.

In a million years there would be many more; for there are a thousand thousand years in one million years. But earth is much older than that—perhaps 4.5 billion years. A billion is one million thousands.

When we say "long ago, perhaps 200 million years ago," we are talking about a time so far back that no one can really understand it. However, geologists have ideas about what the earth was like at that time. Many of them believe that two hundred million years ago there was only one single continent. Geologists have given it the name Pangaea—in Greek, *pan* means all and *gaea* means land. The surface of earth was made of this solitary continent and the sea, a single sea that has been named Panthalassa, from the Greek words for "all sea."

Millions of years ago Pangaea separated into two parts. Geologists do not know why this happened; perhaps it was due to the stresses and strains of a spinning earth, or the heaving of the earth caused by very high lunar tides. It may have been caused by upward movements of hot rock and

11

PANGAEA

LAURASIA

GONDWANA

stone below the earth's surface. However the breakup occurred, they think the pieces moved apart rapidly, perhaps several inches in a single year at first. After some fifty million years Pangaea had become two continents; the northern one has been named Laurasia and the southern one Gondwana, or Gondwanaland. Between them stood the Tethys Sea, an arm of Panthalassa.

During a hundred million years Laurasia and Gondwanaland broke into separate pieces, about twenty of them. The pieces were huge segments called plates. Some of the plates were twenty miles thick; others were much thicker. All were part of the crust of the earth, the outer layer. Each plate floated on hot, soft rock that lay beneath it. The continents we know today—Europe, Asia, Africa, North and South America, and Antarctica—rode atop these plates, and still do. The plates moved, and they are still moving.

Two hundred million years ago North America, Europe, and Asia were probably joined together; so were Australia and Antarctica. India, on a separate plate, was moving northward; Arabia was still joined to Africa.

These super-continents and seas, Gondwanaland, Laurasia, Tethys, Panthalassa, and their movements across the earth surface, remind one of science-fiction stories. And that is precisely what some scientists thought this theory of the earth was. Until a few years ago, that is, when proofs of the existence of mammoth continents, their breakup into several parts, and their movements were revealed.

One proof was the discovery of Lystrosaurus, a dinosaur about the size of a large dog. It was stocky, heavy-skinned, flat-faced, and had no nose at all. Its large eyes were

13

SOUTH
AMERICA

AFRICA

INDIA

ANTARCTICA

AUSTRALIA

LYSTROSAURUS

located high up and far to the front of its blunt, square head. Remains of Lystrosaurus had been found often in India and in South Africa. But in 1967 scientists working in Antarctica made one of the great fossil discoveries when they found remains of Lystrosaurus at a place called Coalsack Bluff.

Paleontologists (scientists who study prehistoric life) had known about this powerful little dinosaur for a long time. They knew that Lystrosaurus had lived in Africa, India, and China some two hundred million years ago. It probably originated on a plate that broke up to form those regions. They also knew that Lystrosaurus was a land animal, and completely unable to have crossed the sea that now separates Africa from Antarctica. The only way the animal could get to Antarctica was over land, which means the migration occurred either at the time when Antarctica was part of a large plate or when there was a land bridge connecting it to such a plate. Many scientists who had strongly questioned the existence of Gondwanaland were now unsure. It looked as though Antarctica, India, and Africa had been joined together at some time during earth's history. Lystrosaurus, a small, obscure short-tailed dinosaur, turned out to be an important key to profound secrets of our planet.

Many discoveries of earth's early history are made under the surface of the sea. This is understandable since most of the earth is covered with water. It was not until the 1920s, though, that scientists learned how to explore the bottom of the sea, and not until the 1950s that they developed reliable equipment for collecting samples from it. Now pipes, sometimes four miles long, are lowered from a ship. Drills at the end of the pipe bore thirty feet or more into the sea floor. The pipe fills with rock and sediment, making a core sample of the sea bottom. During the operation, the ship is held directly above the drill to keep the pipe from breaking. A sound generator is lowered to the ocean bottom right next to the drill. Engines aboard the ship pick up the sounds from the generator and move the ship about, holding it directly above the sound generator.

Samples of the ocean floor brought up in the cores are studied by scientists. They measure the radioactivity of the samples, and the different kinds of minerals they contain. This information enables them to determine the age of the samples. Fossils, or the absence of them, in the core samples reveal much of earth's story, telling when the rocks were formed and whether they were made from silt carried into the sea, or from lava erupted by volcanoes. When hundreds of samples were studied it was found that some parts of the sea floor are much younger than other parts. For example, the youngest part of the Atlantic Ocean floor is along a line extending 12,000 miles north and south called the mid-Atlantic ridge. As the ships moved eastward from the ridge toward Africa, or westward toward South America, the scientists found that the rocks and sediment became older. Let's see what this means.

Some 150 million years ago Gondwanaland began to break into several plates. South America was atop one of them, Africa atop another. Each year the plates drifted apart an inch or so, perhaps even more. The rift between the plates was a weak section of earth's crust. Hot, molten

rock pushed up into the opening, forcing the solid overlying rock into a long, high mountain chain—the mid-Atlantic ridge. Earthquakes occurred there as the plates moved apart, and they still do. Sixty-five million years ago volcanoes became active in the region. As the plates continued to move apart new lava rock formed the high ridges that exist under the sea right now—and are still growing.

The youngest sediments in the Atlantic area are found along, and close to, the mid-Atlantic ridge. Moving east and west of the ridge the sediments become older as distance increases. But none of the undersea sediments and rocks are very old. The oldest was laid down only about 130 million years ago. That's terribly old when we think of a man's lifetime, but it is very young compared with the age of the earth. Rocks have been found recently in Greenland which appear to be 3.98 billion years old— that's 3,980,000,000.

Not only do the ages of rocks and sediments tell us about the early earth, but so also does the magnetism of rocks. Earth has a magnetic field. You see an effect of this when a compass needle points north and south. If a piece of iron lies in a north-south line for a few years, earth's magnetism causes the iron to become magnetized—the iron crystals form into a north-south line. So it is with rocks. Earth's magnetic field causes certain rock crystals to form in a north-south line. If there should be a change in earth's magnetism, there would be a change in the pattern of the rock crystals. By studying carefully the arrangement of rock crystals, geologists can learn the history of the rocks and

MID-ATLANTIC RIDGE

A section through the
Mid-Atlantic Ridge, showing
magnetic field pattern.

the history of the part of the earth where the rocks are found. They know, for example, that the present north magnetic pole of the earth used to be the south magnetic pole. In fact, the poles of the earth have shifted back and forth, exchanged locations, at least 171 times during recent earth history—back about 76 million years.

Sensitive meters for measuring magnetism were towed along the ocean floor by ships, and the information they gathered was used to make maps and charts of ancient magnetic fields. The pattern on one side of a rift, the region between two plates, is repeated identically on the other side. Rocks having the same pattern must have been

19

connected when the pattern was forming. The magnetic patterns which were produced in rocks of North America and England millions of years ago, and which persist today, would match perfectly if the two regions were joined together.

South America and Africa were joined at one time. The bulge of South America fits perfectly into the hollow of

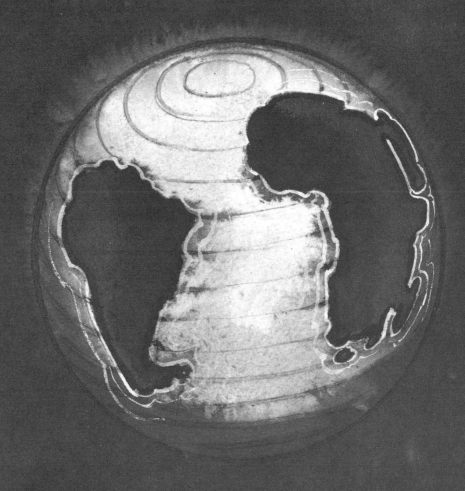

Africa; and the mid-Atlantic ridge, the line of separation between the two continents, parallels the west coast of Africa. Right now the two continents are drifting away from each other at the rate of an inch a year. Africa is moving east and north, and South America toward the west and slightly north. Fifty million years from now the continents will be a thousand miles farther apart than they are now.

Mountains

In the next fifty million years movements of the plates will probably have caused other gigantic changes. India will push northward, dig under the Asian plate, and push it upward. The Himalaya mountains, which were formed when India moved northward millions of years ago, will rise even higher than they do now. These mountains were pushed up from the sea. We know this because fossils of creatures that lived under the sea are found atop the Himalayas. Japan, Siberia, and Eastern Asia will push south-eastward into the Pacific Basin.

In the future, scientists believe that the Mediterranean Sea will be a fraction of its present size, for it will have been squeezed together as the Africa plate moves northward. The Alps will be higher than they are now. Arabia will push north and east; huge chunks will break away from Africa;

22

and Australia will bump into Indonesia. In North America, Los Angeles will be far north of where San Francisco now is, perhaps as far north as the Aleutian Islands. Los Angeles will ride on a thin slab of western United States (the edge of the Pacific plate) which will break free of the continent.

Earth is a restless planet. As huge masses of the crust move, earthquakes are produced. Plates scrape against one another, and the earth rumbles and shakes, the edges disappearing into the magma that lies beneath the crust. Most earthquakes are small tremors caused by unnoticed motions of limited masses. We are usually not aware of them, but they register on seismometers, sensitive instruments that record slight motions of the crust. Sometimes huge masses slide a foot or more. The quake that results may destroy whole cities and kill thousands of people.

23

Where there are earthquakes there are almost always volcanoes, vents in the crust of the earth. Hot molten rock spurts into the air, or into the sea if the volcano is under water. Mountains appear where there had been level plains. Whole islands may be created.

Iceland is part of the mid-Atlantic ridge. It is a country wracked by earthquakes and volcanoes; fourteen volcanic eruptions already in this century. In November 1963 the sea off the Vestmann Islands in southern Iceland boiled and spouted. Columns of steam rose high into the air as red-hot lava pushed upward from the bottom of the sea. Ashes exploded skyward. Rapidly the ashes accumulated, and an island was born. The wind and sea bore the ashes away, but more ashes piled up. Hot lava reached the top and made a hard surface covering the ashes. In a few days the volcano was 130 feet above sea level, and a third of a mile long. A month later the mountain was 500 feet high and half a mile across. For months the lava flowed upward, adding an acre a day to the island. Today a small island, a bit over a square mile in area, is cooling down. The pounding sea is rounding off the jagged lava. Seeds carried by the sea, by wind and sea birds, are sprouting into plants. The island is called Surtsey after Surtur, a mythological Icelandic giant who brought fire to the land and fought against other gods. It is a new island, among the newest on the earth, an outcropping of the mid-Atlantic ridge.

The island of Hawaii is part of a chain made from lava that flowed out of an active volcano, a large opening in the crust of the earth. Seventy million years ago the lava formed huge cones under the sea, cones that often broke

the surface and became islands. The lava kept flowing and, as old cones were carried northward, new cones were created. Now in the Pacific Ocean there is a chain of volcanic cones 3,700 miles long. The one farthest north is the oldest, and as we get closer to Hawaii the cones become younger. Today lava is still flowing under Hawaii.

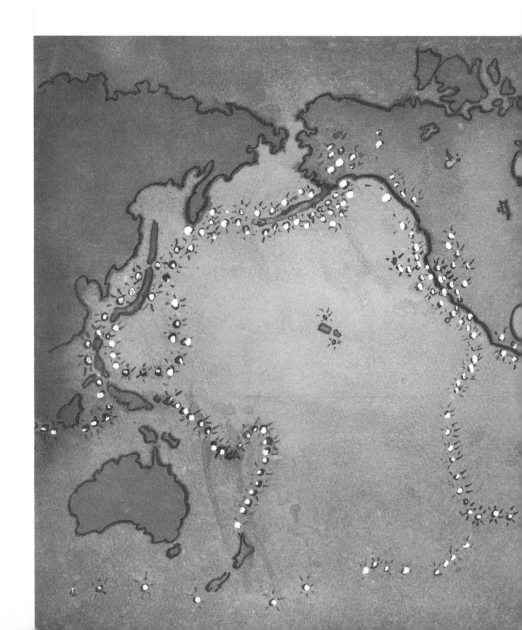

The island is being carried northward, moving with the Pacific plate. Eventually, Hawaii will move away from the volcanic openings in the earth, and new cones will grow where Hawaii now stands.

The map of the earth shows the Pacific plate, and the other plates into which the crust is divided. The dots are

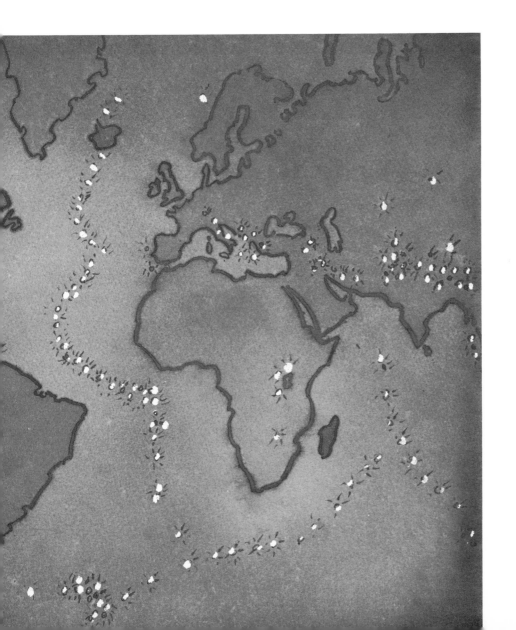

the centers of recent earthquakes; all of them occurred since 1950. Most earthquakes happen along the edges of the plates. Indeed, the rifts at the edges of plates are centers of continuous activity. Lava from the deep layers of the earth flows into them. In some places the edges of one plate dig under another and disappear into the magma. The upper plate is folded and raised, forming the mountains of the world. In other places plates rub against one another, scraping and sliding an inch a year and as much as four or five inches in some locations.

The plates are moving now and they will continue to move. Fifty million years from now the continents will have shifted so much that the world will look quite different from the way it now appears.

Even during a short period, earth will change; volcanoes will erupt producing mountains and islands, earth layers will slide and there will be disastrous earthquakes. During your lifetime the distance between the United States and Europe will become six feet greater, Hawaii will be several feet farther north, Los Angeles will be ten feet closer to San Francisco. No matter where you live the earth beneath you is moving. Earth is a restless planet, always moving, always changing.

Bibliography

Asimov, Isaac, *The Double Planet.* New York: Abelard-Schuman, 1960.

Branley, Franklyn M., *The Earth: Planet Number Three.* New York: Thomas Y. Crowell, 1966.

Gamow, George, *A Planet Called Earth.* New York: Viking Press, 1963.

Lauber, Patricia, *This Restless Earth.* New York: Random House, 1970.

Strahler, Arthur N., *The Earth Sciences.* New York: Harper & Row, 1963.

29

Index

31

ABOUT THE AUTHOR

Franklyn M. Branley, Astronomer Emeritus and former Chairman of The American Museum-Hayden Planetarium, is well known as the author of many books about astronomy and other sciences for young people of all ages. He is also co-editor of the Let's-Read-and-Find-Out Science books.

Dr. Branley holds degrees from New York University, Columbia University, and the State University of New York College at New Paltz. He and his wife live in Woodcliff Lake, New Jersey.

ABOUT THE ARTIST

Daniel Maffia was born in France and came to the United States when he was twelve. He received his Master of Fine Arts degree from Pratt Institute in Brooklyn and has taught at Sarah Lawrence College. Mr. Maffia's work has been exhibited in several one-man shows, and commissioned by leading magazines and book publishers. He lives in Fort Lee, New Jersey and has his studio in Englewood.

551   6496
B
Branley, Franklyn M.
Shakes, Quakes, And Shifts

DATE DUE		
JAN 19 '78		
MAY 28 '79		
FEB 5 '81		
OCT 27 '81		
NOV 3 '81		
APR 23 '85		
JAN 12 '88		
JAN 19 '88		
NOV 13 '88		
1/24/91		
FEB 14 '91		
MAR 15 '91		